HAL LEONARD

BOOK ONE

GUITAR
TAB METHOD

Written by Jeff Schroedl

Contributing Editors: Jeff Arnold, Kurt Plahna, and Jim Schustedt

PLAYBACK+
Speed • Pitch • Balance • Loop

To access audio visit:
www.halleonard.com/mylibrary

Enter Code
7449-9605-8216-9563

ISBN 978-1-61774-260-6

Visit Hal Leonard Online at
www.halleonard.com

Contact Us:
Hal Leonard
7777 West Bluemound Road
Milwaukee, WI 53213
Email: info@halleonard.com

In Europe contact:
Hal Leonard Europe Limited
42 Wigmore Street
Marylebone, London, W1U 2RN
Email: info@halleonardeurope.com

In Australia contact:
Hal Leonard Australia Pty. Ltd.
4 Lentara Court
Cheltenham, Victoria, 3192 Australia
Email: info@halleonard.com.au

GETTING STARTED

PARTS OF THE GUITAR

This method is designed for use with an electric or acoustic guitar. Both are tuned the same, contain the same notes, and have mostly the same parts. The main difference is that acoustic guitars have a soundhole and are loud enough to be played without amplification, while electric guitars are plugged into an amp.

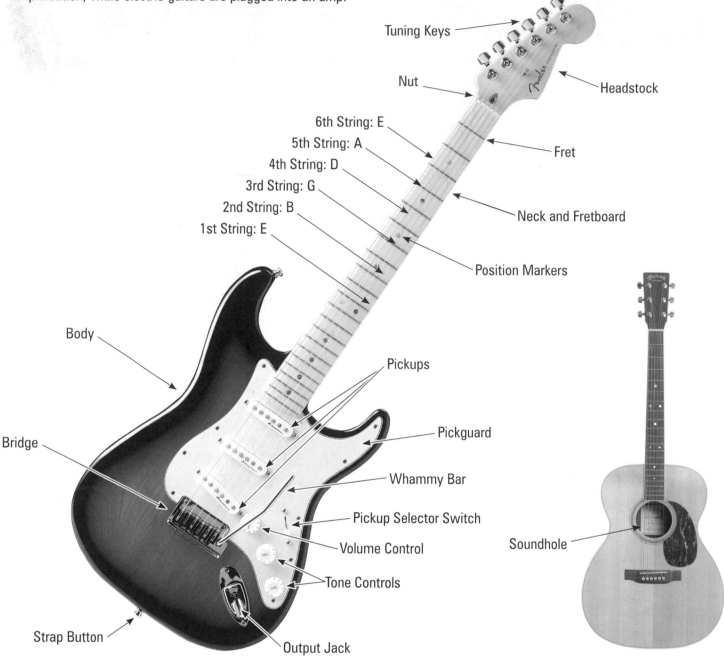

Tuning Keys

Nut

Headstock

6th String: E

5th String: A

Fret

4th String: D

3rd String: G

2nd String: B

Neck and Fretboard

1st String: E

Position Markers

Body

Pickups

Bridge

Pickguard

Whammy Bar

Soundhole

Pickup Selector Switch

Volume Control

Tone Controls

Strap Button

Output Jack

TUNING

The quickest and most accurate way to get in tune is to use an electronic tuner. You can either plug your guitar into the tuner or use the tuner's built-in microphone to tune an acoustic.

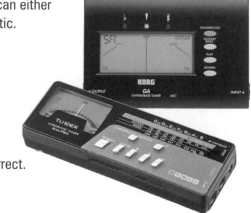

The guitar's six open strings should be tuned to these pitches:

E (thickest)–A–D–G–B–E (thinnest)

If you twist a string's tuning key clockwise, the pitch will become lower; if you twist the tuning key counterclockwise, the pitch will become higher.

Adjust the tuning keys until the electronic tuner's meter indicates that the pitch is correct. Or, listen to each string's correct pitch on the first audio track and slowly turn the tuning key until the sound of the string matches the sound on the track.

HOLDING THE GUITAR

Use the pictures below to help find a comfortable playing position. Whether you decide to sit or stand, it's important to remain relaxed and tension-free.

LEFT-HAND POSITION

Fingers are numbered 1 through 4. Arch your fingers and press the strings down firmly between the frets with your fingertips only.

Place your thumb on the underside of the guitar neck. Avoid letting the palm of your hand touch the neck of the guitar.

RIGHT-HAND POSITION

Hold the pick between your thumb and index finger. Strike the string with a downward motion approximately halfway between the bridge and neck.

The fingers not holding the pick may rest on the guitar for extra support.

THE LOW E STRING

Guitar music is written in a form of notation called **tablature**, or **tab** for short. Each line represents a string, and each number represents a fret. The thickest string played open, or not pressed, is the low E note. In tab, an open string is represented with a zero (0). The note F is located on the 1st fret. Press, or "fret" the string with your 1st finger, directly behind the first metal fret.

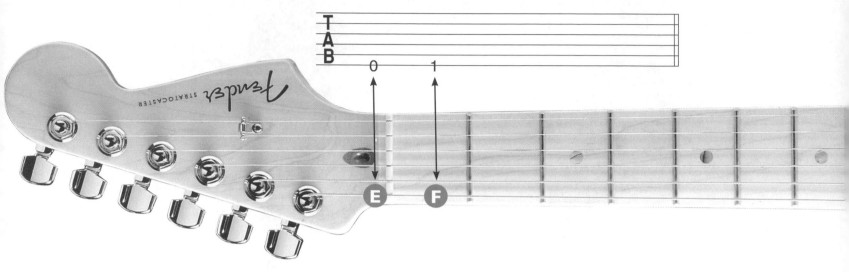

Play the theme from the movie *Jaws* using the notes E and F. Attack the string with a downstroke of the pick. Speed up as the numbers get closer together.

THEME FROM "JAWS"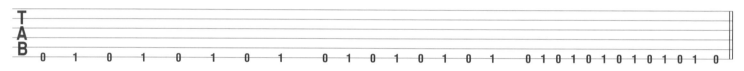

By John Williams
Copyright © 1975 USI B MUSIC PUBLISHING   Copyright Renewed   All Rights Controlled and Administered by SONGS OF UNIVERSAL, INC.

Now let's learn more notes on the low E string.

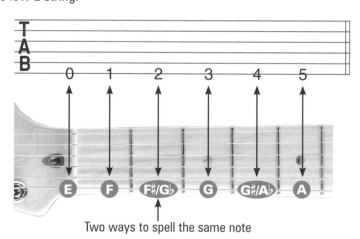

Two ways to spell the same note

GREEN ONIONS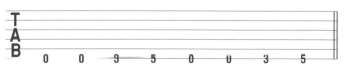

"Green Onions" by Booker T. & the MG's uses the notes E, G, and A. Follow the tab and pick the notes at a steady speed, or **tempo**.

Written by Al Jackson, Jr., Lewis Steinberg, Booker T. Jones and Steve Cropper
© 1962 (Renewed 1990) AL JACKSON JR. MUSIC (BMI)/Administered by BUG MUSIC and IRVING MUSIC, INC.

PETER GUNN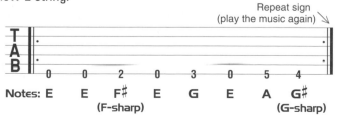

A **riff** is a short, composed phrase that is repeated. The popular riff from "Peter Gunn" is played with notes on the low E string.

Repeat sign
(play the music again)

Notes: E   E   F#   E   G   E   A   G#
            (F-sharp)   (G-sharp)

Theme Song from The Television Series   By Henry Mancini
Copyright © 1958 NORTHRIDGE MUSIC CO.   Copyright Renewed
All Rights Controlled and Administered by UNIVERSAL MUSIC CORP.

THE A STRING

Here are the notes within the first five frets of the 5th string, called the A string.

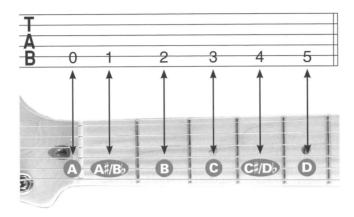

BRIT ROCK

This catchy riff uses the notes A, B, and C.

LEAN ON ME

This song was a #1 hit in two decades. It uses the notes A, B, C#, and D.

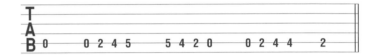

RHYTHM TAB

Rhythm Tab adds rhythmic values to the basic tab staff. **Bar lines** divide music into **measures**. A **time signature** tells how many beats are in each measure and what kind of note is counted as one beat. In 4/4 time ("four-four"), there are four beats in each measure, and a **quarter note** is counted as one beat. It has a vertical stem joined to the tab number.

FEEL THE BEAT

Count "1, 2, 3, 4" as you play.

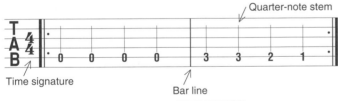

WORKING MAN

This classic riff by the band Rush uses quarter notes on strings 5 and 6.

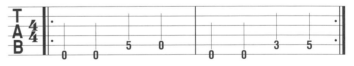

ZEPPELIN TRIBUTE

Anchor the palm of your pick hand on the bridge of the guitar to help your picking accuracy.

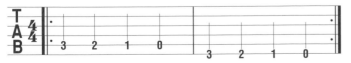

BLUES RIFF

Use the 3rd finger of your fret hand for notes on the 4th fret, 1st finger for the note on the 2nd fret, and 4th finger (pinky) for the note on the 5th fret.

MORE RIFFS

The next two riffs are written in **3/4 time**. This means there are three beats in each measure, and a quarter note receives one beat.

MY NAME IS JONAS

Count "1–2–3, 1–2–3" as you play this riff by the band Weezer.

MALAGUEÑA

This traditional Spanish piece is very popular among classical guitarists.

A **half note** lasts two beats. It fills the time of two quarter notes. In tab, a circle surrounds the tab number(s) and is attached to a vertical stem.

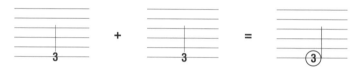

CANON IN D

The first line is played with half notes and the second line is played with quarter notes. Count aloud and keep a steady tempo.

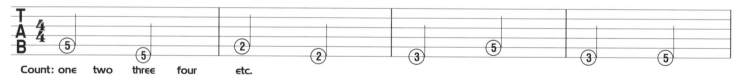

ELECTRIC FUNERAL

The heavy metal band Black Sabbath used half notes and quarter notes for this powerful, eerie riff.

COOL GROOVE

Now try playing half notes in 3/4 time.

An **eighth note** lasts half a beat, or half as long as a quarter note. One eighth note is written with a stem and flag; consecutive eighth notes are connected with a beam.

LADY MADONNA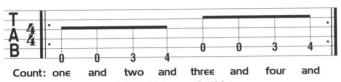

While playing this Beatles classic, count with the word "and" between the beats.

Count: one and two and three and four and

CRAZY TRAIN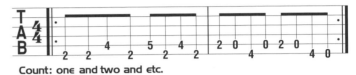

Randy Rhoads played the driving, eighth-note guitar riff on this immortal Ozzy Osbourne song.

Count: one and two and etc.

AQUALUNG

Now let's mix eighth notes and quarter notes on this famous Jethro Tull song.

GREEN-EYED LADY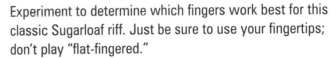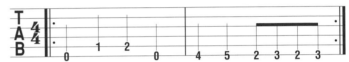

Experiment to determine which fingers work best for this classic Sugarloaf riff. Just be sure to use your fingertips; don't play "flat-fingered."

A **rest** is a symbol used to indicate silence in music. In 4/4 time, a **quarter rest** fills the time of one beat and a **half rest** fills the time of two beats.

Quarter Rest
One Beat

Half Rest
Two Beats

25 OR 6 TO 4

This riff by the band Chicago uses a quarter rest. Mute the string by touching it gently with the palm of your picking hand. You can also release the pressure of your fret hand to silence the string.

Count: one and two and three (four)

BRAIN STEW

The band Green Day used a similar descending pattern for this hit song, which uses quarter and half rests.

Count: one and (two) (three - four)

THE D STRING

Here are the notes within the first five frets of the 4th string, called the D string.

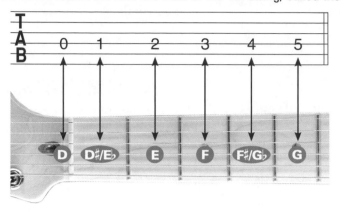

D-MENTED

Say the note names aloud as you play this sinister riff.

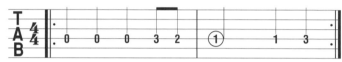

Copyright © 2012 by HAL LEONARD CORPORATION

MACHINE GUN

Jimi Hendrix used this riff as the foundation for his song from the album *Band of Gypsys*. The dot above beat 3 is called a **staccato** mark. It tells you to cut the note short.

Words and Music by Jimi Hendrix
Copyright © 1970 by EXPERIENCE HENDRIX, L.L.C. Copyright Renewed 1998
All Rights Controlled and Administered by EXPERIENCE HENDRIX, L.L.C.

OH, PRETTY WOMAN

This Roy Orbison song features one of the most recognizable riffs of all time.

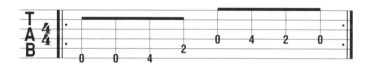

Words and Music by Roy Orbison and Bill Dees
Copyright © 1964 (Renewed 1992) ROY ORBISON MUSIC COMPANY, BARBARA ORBISON MUSIC COMPANY and
SONY/ATV MUSIC PUBLISHING LLC
All Rights on behalf of ROY ORBISON MUSIC COMPANY and BARBARA ORBISON MUSIC COMPANY Administered by
BMG CHRYSALIS
All Rights on behalf of SONY/ATV MUSIC PUBLISHING LLC Administered by SONY/ATV MUSIC PUBLISHING LLC, 8
Music Square West, Nashville, TN 37203

YOU GIVE LOVE A BAD NAME

As you play this Bon Jovi riff, use the side or heel of your pick hand to muffle the strings. This technique is called **palm muting** (P.M.).

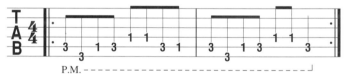

Words and Music by Jon Bon Jovi, Desmond Child and Richie Sambora
Copyright © 1986 UNIVERSAL - POLYGRAM INTERNATIONAL PUBLISHING, INC., BON JOVI PUBLISHING, SONY/ATV
MUSIC PUBLISHING LLC and AGGRESSIVE MUSIC
All Rights for BON JOVI PUBLISHING Controlled and Administered by UNIVERSAL - POLYGRAM INTERNATIONAL
PUBLISHING, INC.
All Rights for SONY/ATV MUSIC PUBLISHING LLC and AGGRESSIVE MUSIC Administered by SONY/ATV MUSIC
PUBLISHING LLC, 8 Music Square West, Nashville, TN 37203

A **tie** is a curved, dashed line connecting two notes of the same pitch. It tells you not to strike the second note. The first note should be struck and held for the combined value of both notes.

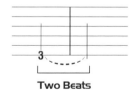

Two Beats

Three Beats

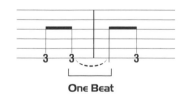

One Beat

SPACE TRUCKIN'

You're now ready to tackle this driving riff from the band Deep Purple.

Words and Music by Ritchie Blackmore, Ian Gillan, Roger Glover, Jon Lord and Ian Paice
© 1972 (Renewed 2000) B. FELDMAN & CO. LTD. trading as HEC MUSIC
All Rights for the United States and Canada Controlled and Administered by GLENWOOD MUSIC CORP.

MONEY (THAT'S WHAT I WANT)

"Money" has been recorded by countless artists, including Barrett Strong, the Beatles, Buddy Guy, and Waylon Jennings.

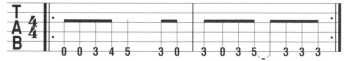

Words and Music by Berry Gordy and Janie Bradford
© 1959 (Renewed 1987) JOBETE MUSIC CO., INC.
All Rights Controlled and Administered by EMI APRIL MUSIC INC. and EMI BLACKWOOD MUSIC INC. on behalf of
JOBETE MUSIC CO., INC. and STONE AGATE MUSIC (A Division of JOBETE MUSIC CO., INC.)

An **eighth rest** indicates to be silent for half a beat. It looks like this: ⅞

HAVA NAGILA

Start slowly and use your pinky for the G♯ on the 4th fret.

Count: one two (three) and four and

SUPER FREAK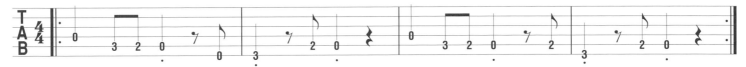

This funky Rick James hit uses both eighth and quarter rests.

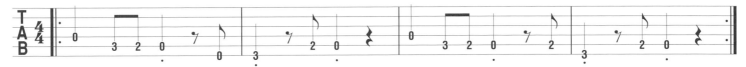

JAMIE'S CRYIN'

This Van Halen riff uses both eighth rests and ties.

DAY TRIPPER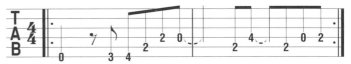

On this Beatles classic, you'll get a workout on all three bottom strings.

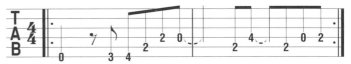

The next riffs begin with **pickup notes**. Count pickup notes as if they were the last portion of a full measure.

YOU REALLY GOT ME

Van Halen covered this Kinks song on their first album.

and one and two and (three) (four) and

COME AS YOU ARE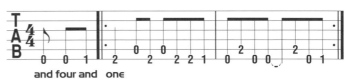

This Nirvana riff begins on the "and" of beat 3.

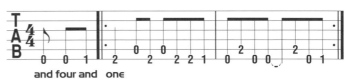

and four and one

MISSISSIPPI QUEEN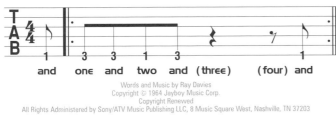

A wavy line over a note indicates to apply **vibrato**, a technique produced by pulling (bending) and releasing a string in rapid succession.

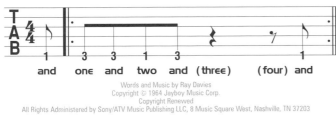

FEEL YOUR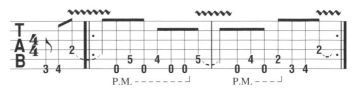
LOVE TONIGHT

Here's another Van Halen riff. This one applies palm muting and vibrato.

P.M. --------- ‖ P.M. ---- ‖

WIPE OUT

Now it's time to play your first complete song. "Wipe Out" is one of the most popular instrumental hits of all time. It was originally recorded by the Surfaris in 1963 and has been performed since by numerous groups, including the Ventures and the Beach Boys.

During the famous drum breakdown in the second half of the song, you'll notice a **whole rest**. It indicates one full measure of silence, and looks like this:

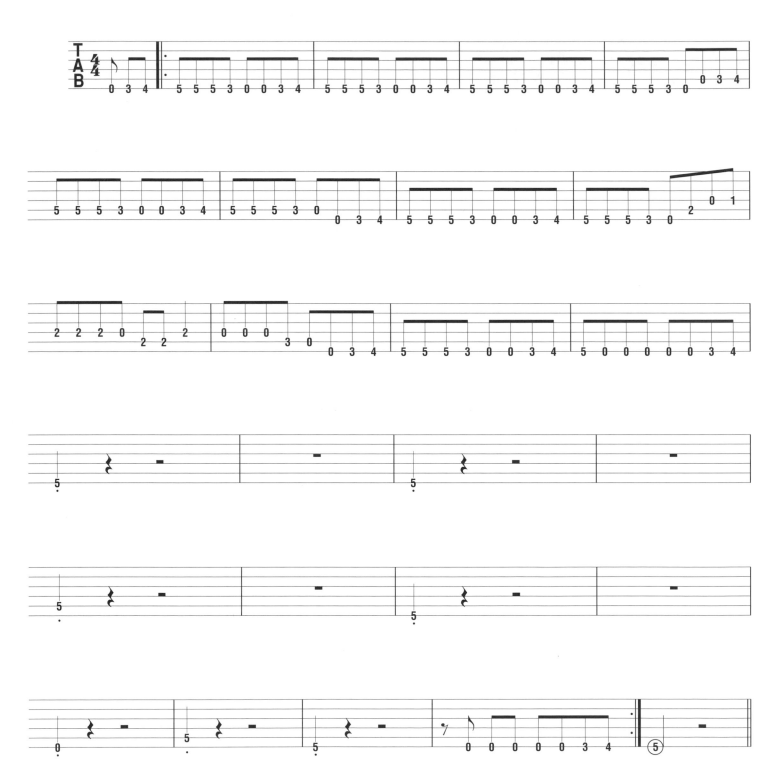

POWER CHORDS

A **power chord** consists of two notes played together. Rock guitarists use power chords to create a low, powerful sound.

The lower note of a power chord is called the **root note**. It is the note upon which the chord is named. The power chord label also includes the suffix "5."

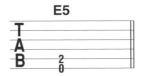

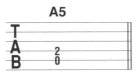

METALLIC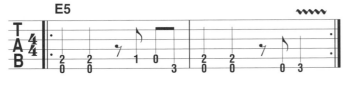

Attack both notes of the power chord at the same time with a single downstroke.

JACK HAMMER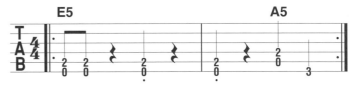

Remember to stop the chords from ringing when you see rests or staccato dots.

T.N.T.

Australian hard rock band AC/DC uses power chords in many songs, including this classic riff from "T.N.T."

Words and Music by Angus Young, Malcolm Young and Bon Scott

MOVABLE POWER CHORDS

Power chords can be played up and down the lower strings of the guitar fretboard using one simple fingering shape. Use your 1st and 3rd fingers as shown below.

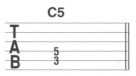

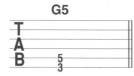

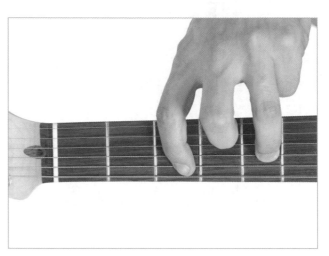

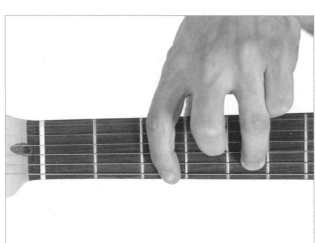

A power chord's name comes from its root note, or where your 1st finger is placed on the fretboard. Here is a diagram of the notes you've learned so far within the first five frets of strings 5 and 6, and the power chords built upon these roots.

ROOT ON 6TH STRING

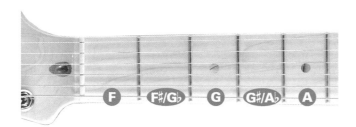

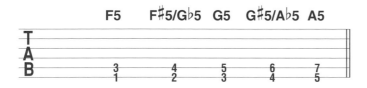

ROOT ON 5TH STRING

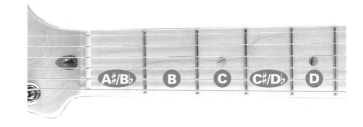

ALL ALONG THE WATCHTOWER

Bob Dylan, Jimi Hendrix, and others have recorded this song. The root note of all three power chords is on the 6th string.

MEGA-HEAVY

This riff chugs on the low E string between power chord attacks.

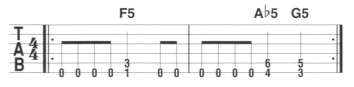

SMELLS LIKE TEEN SPIRIT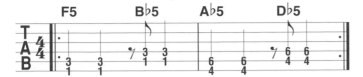

This Nirvana hit uses power chords with roots on the 5th and 6th strings.

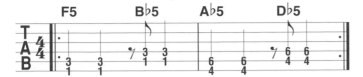

I CAN'T EXPLAIN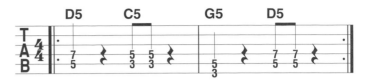

Guitarist Pete Townshend of the Who used power chords in many songs, including "I Can't Explain."

When a **dot** appears after a note, you extend the note by half its value. A **dotted half note** lasts for three beats.

A **whole note** is twice as long as a half note; it lasts four beats. A whole note is written in a circle with no stem.

BABA O'RILEY

Now let's mix movable and open power chords to play another rock classic by the Who.

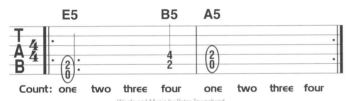

OWNER OF A LONELY HEART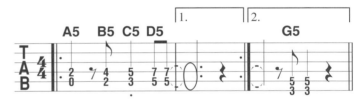

This riff by the band Yes is tabbed with **ending brackets**. The 1st time through, play the 1st ending and repeat as usual. The 2nd time, skip the 1st ending and play the 2nd ending.

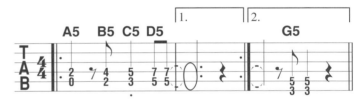

JAILBREAK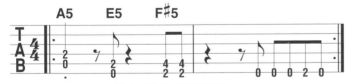

Power chords are often mixed with single notes. Try this riff popularized by the band Thin Lizzy.

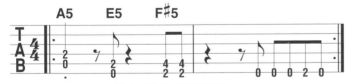

REFUGEE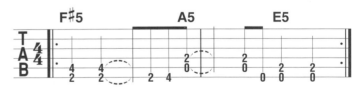

Tom Petty's "Refugee" also puts power chords and single notes to good use.

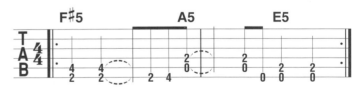

BATMAN THEME

Here's an easy, fun riff that is a variation of the open A5 power chord.

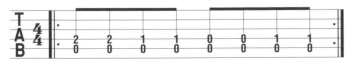

CHICAGO BLUES

Blues guitarists commonly enhance simple power chords in a manner similar to this rhythm figure.

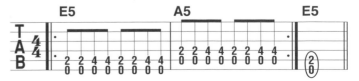

WILD THING

"Wild Thing" is one of rock music's most enduring songs. Originally a #1 hit for the Troggs in 1966, it has since been recorded by Jimi Hendrix, Sam Kinison, and many others. The entire song can be played using movable power chords.

Intro

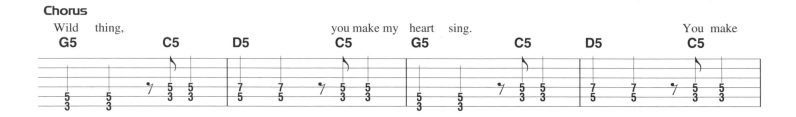

Chorus

Wild thing,   you make my heart sing.   You make

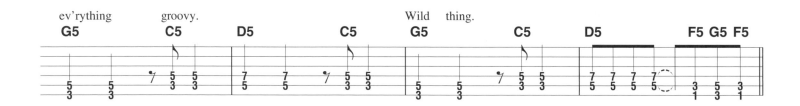

ev'rything   groovy.   Wild thing.

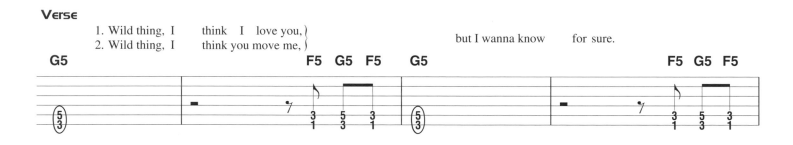

Verse

1. Wild thing, I   think   I   love you,   but I wanna know   for sure.
2. Wild thing, I   think you move me,

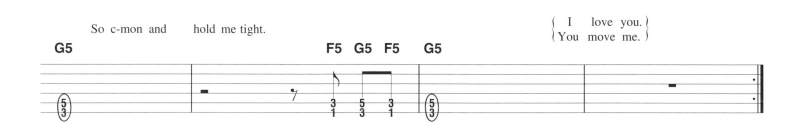

So c-mon and   hold me tight.   { I   love you. / You   move me. }

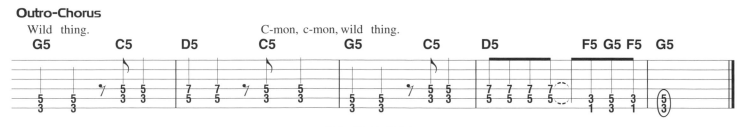

Outro-Chorus

Wild thing.   C-mon, c-mon, wild thing.

Words and Music by Chip Taylor
© 1965 (Renewed 1993) EMI BLACKWOOD MUSIC INC.

CHECKPOINT

You're halfway through this book and well on your way to a rewarding hobby or a successful career with the guitar. Let's take a moment to review some of what you've learned so far.

NOTE NAMES

Draw a line to match each note on the left with its correct name on the right.

  C

  B

  G

  E

  F

  A

  D

SYMBOLS & TERMS

Draw a line to match each symbol on the left with its correct name on the right.

  Palm Mute

P.M. Half Note

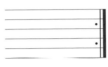 Eighth Rest

  Quarter Rest

A5 Eighth Note

  Repeat Sign

  Power Chord

Write the note names in the spaces provided.

Add bar lines.

Below the tab staff are note names. Write the notes on the tab staff.

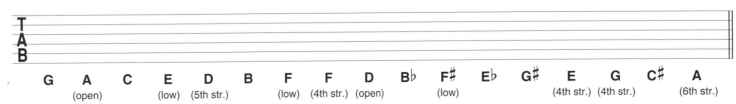

THE G STRING

Here are the notes within the first five frets of the 3rd string, called the G string.

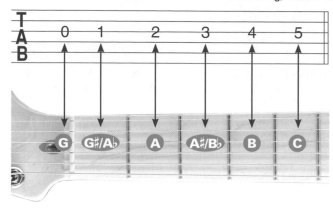

NORWEGIAN WOOD (THIS BIRD HAS FLOWN)

This Indian-influenced Beatles song, written in 3/4 time, was the first rock song to feature a sitar on a recording.

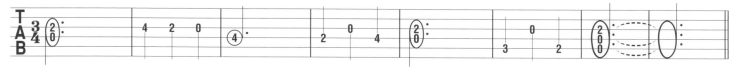

DON'T FEAR THE REAPER

In some songs, like this cowbell-infused classic by Blue Öyster Cult, it's common to see the instruction "**let ring**." Instead of releasing your fingers after each note is played, you hold them down, allowing the notes to sustain.

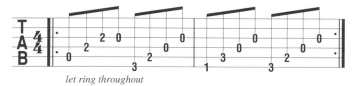

let ring throughout

LA BAMBA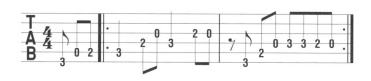

This song has been recorded by Ritchie Valens, Los Lobos, and many others. It uses notes on all four strings you've learned so far. Use your 2nd finger to press the notes on the 2nd fret and 3rd finger on the 3rd fret.

SMOKE ON THE WATER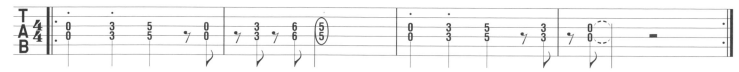

Deep Purple's "Smoke on the Water" features one of the greatest rock riffs of all time. Strike the two-note chords, or **dyads**, with downstrokes. Although you haven't learned notes beyond the 5th fret, simply use your 3rd finger to press the notes on the 6th fret.

PIPELINE

"Pipeline" is a classic guitar instrumental. The original version was a surf-rock hit for the Chantays in 1963, and it has since been recorded by the Ventures, Dick Dale, Stevie Ray Vaughan, and others. It uses single notes on the bottom four strings, as well as a few power chords. In the A section, fret the B note (5th string, 2nd fret) for the entire four measures.

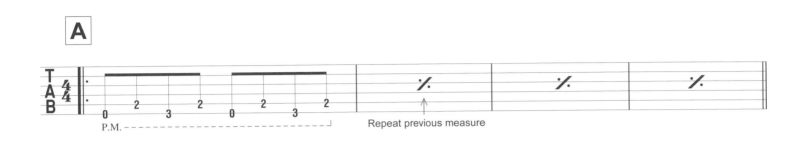

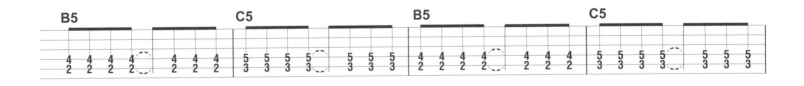

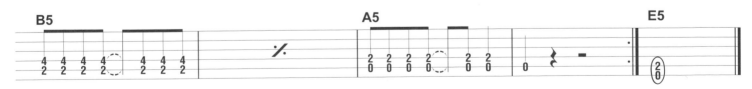

By Bob Spickard and Brian Carman
Copyright © 1962, 1963 (Renewed) by Regent Music Corporation (BMI)

THE B STRING

Here are the notes within the first five frets of the 2nd string, called the B string.

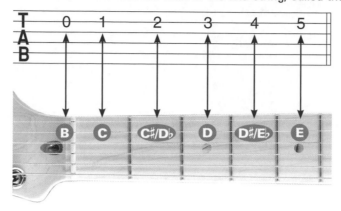

DUELIN' BANJOS

This bluegrass theme was featured in the movie *Deliverance*.

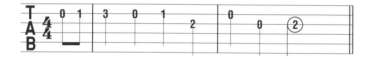

SUSIE-Q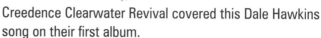

Creedence Clearwater Revival covered this Dale Hawkins song on their first album.

slight P.M. throughout

FÜR ELISE

This instantly recognizable piece in 3/4 time is truly a classic. Beethoven wrote it in 1810.

WALK DON'T RUN

The Ventures, Chet Atkins, and others have recorded this popular instrumental song.

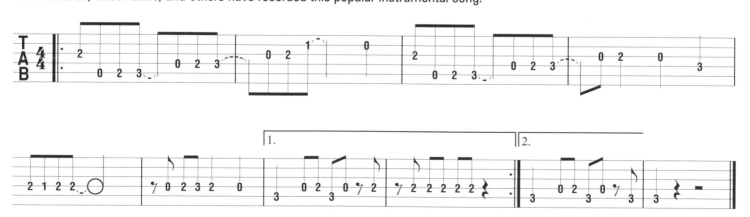

THE HIGH E STRING

Here are the notes within the first five frets of the 1st string, called the E string.

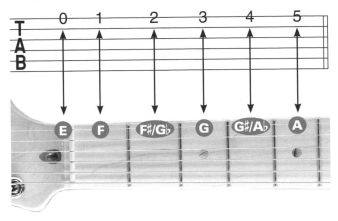

IN MY LIFE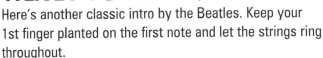

The opening riff of this song by the Beatles uses notes on the top two strings. Fret-hand fingerings are indicated below the tab staff.

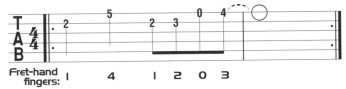

Fret-hand fingers: 1 4 1 2 0 3

Words and Music by John Lennon and Paul McCartney
Copyright © 1965 Sony/ATV Music Publishing LLC
Copyright Renewed
All Rights Administered by Sony/ATV Music Publishing LLC, 8 Music Square West, Nashville, TN 37203

TICKET TO RIDE

Here's another classic intro by the Beatles. Keep your 1st finger planted on the first note and let the strings ring throughout.

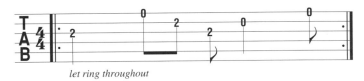

let ring throughout

Words and Music by John Lennon and Paul McCartney
Copyright © 1965 Sony/ATV Music Publishing LLC
Copyright Renewed
All Rights Administered by Sony/ATV Music Publishing LLC, 8 Music Square West, Nashville, TN 37203

REBEL, REBEL

To play this David Bowie riff, follow the "let ring" indications and be sure to mute the low E note in the 2nd measure with your palm.

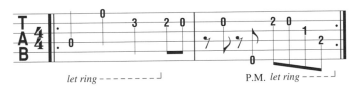

let ring — — — — — — — —   P.M. *let ring* — — — —

Words and Music by David Bowie
© 1974 (Renewed 2002) EMI MUSIC PUBLISHING LTD., JONES MUSIC AMERICA and CHRYSALIS MUSIC
All Rights for EMI MUSIC PUBLISHING LTD. Controlled and Administered by COLGEMS-EMI MUSIC INC.
All Rights for JONES MUSIC AMERICA Administered by ARZO PUBLISHING
All Rights for CHRYSALIS MUSIC Administered by BMG RIGHTS MANAGEMENT (US) LLC

SUNDAY BLOODY SUNDAY

Now play this riff by the band U2, paying close attention to the fingerings below the tab. Keep the notes depressed so they ring, and lay your 1st finger across the top three strings at the 2nd fret for the last half of measure 1.

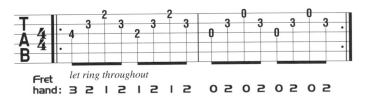

let ring throughout

Fret hand: 3 2 1 2 1 2 0 2 0 2 0 2

Words and Music by U2
Copyright © 1983 UNIVERSAL MUSIC PUBLISHING INTERNATIONAL B.V.
All Rights in the United States and Canada Controlled and Administered by
UNIVERSAL - POLYGRAM INTERNATIONAL PUBLISHING, INC.

FOXEY LADY

Here is one of Jimi Hendrix's signature riffs. Lay your pinky across the top two strings to play the notes at the 5th fret.

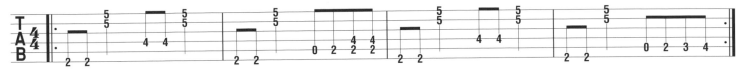

Words and Music by Jimi Hendrix
Copyright © 1967, 1968, 1980 EXPERIENCE HENDRIX, L.L.C.
Copyright Renewed 1995, 1996
All Rights Controlled and Administered by EXPERIENCE HENDRIX, L.L.C.

JAMES BOND THEME

DEMO   MINUS GTR. 1   MINUS GTR. 2

The main theme of the James Bond films is powerful, mysterious, and instantly recognizable. It contains notes on all six strings, and is arranged here as a duet for two guitars. Pick a part and play!

Once you've reached the end of section E, you'll see the instructions "D.S. al Coda (no repeat)." Jump back to the sign (𝄋) at letter B and play up to the instruction "To Coda." At this point, jump to the last line of the tune where it's labeled "Coda," and play the final five measures.

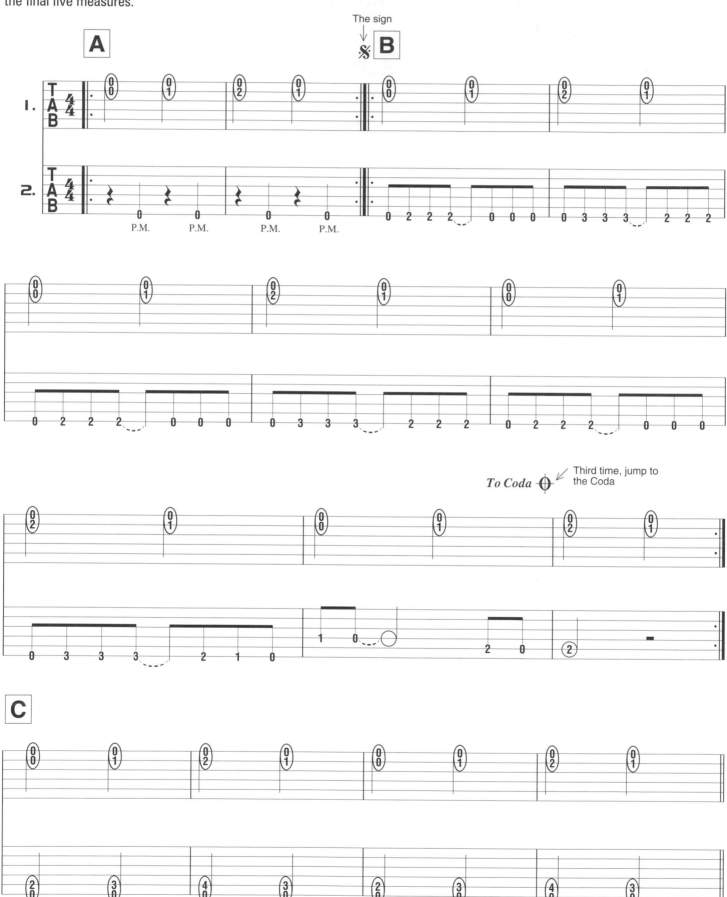

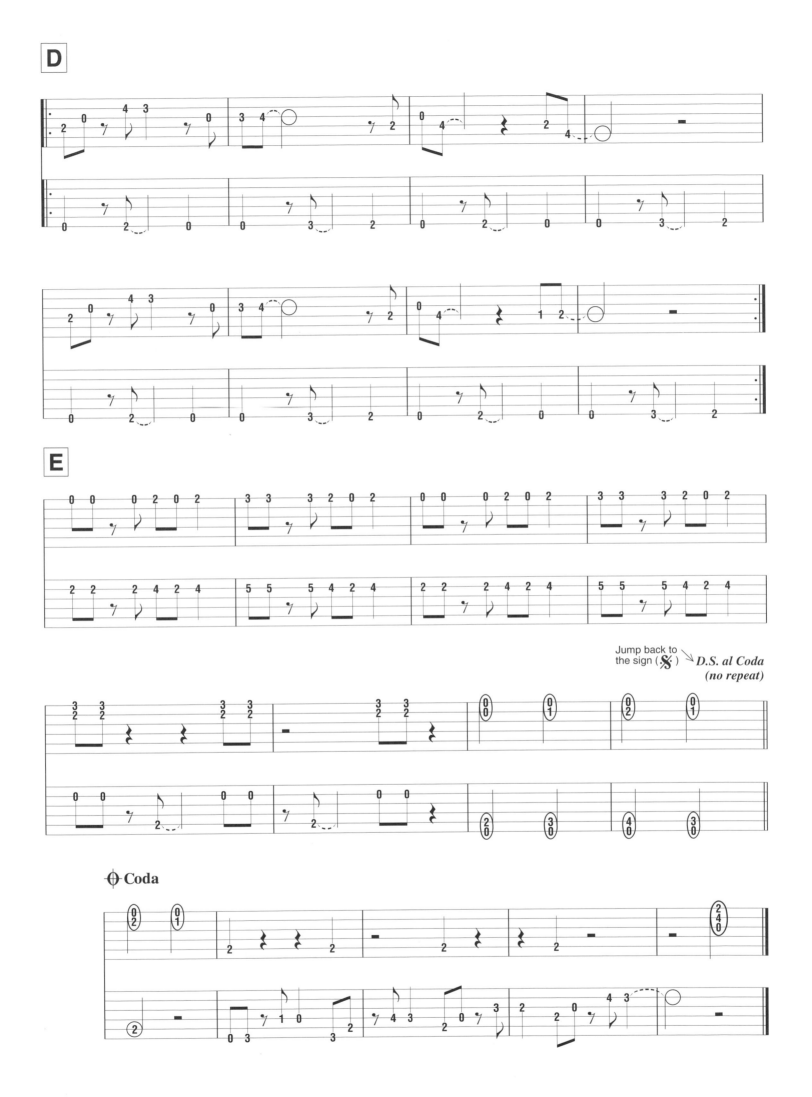

OPEN CHORDS

Chords that contain open strings are called open-position chords, or simply **open chords**. They are used for accompaniment, or **rhythm guitar**, and usually incorporate four, five, or all six strings.

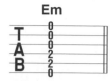

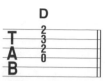

GET UP STAND UP 🔊

Playing chords in a rhythmic pattern is called **strumming**. Strum the E minor chord in a downward motion to play a basic version of this Bob Marley song.

1. Get up,   stand up.   Stand up   for   your right.
2. Get up,   stand up.   Don't   give up   the fight.

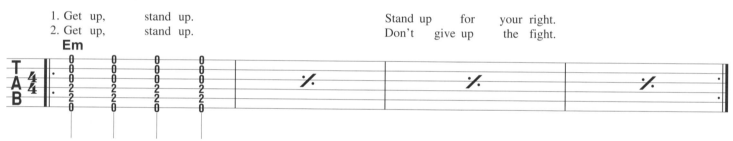

Words and Music by Bob Marley and Peter Tosh
Copyright © 1974 Fifty-Six Hope Road Music Ltd., Odnil Music Ltd., State One Music America LLC and Embassy Music Corporation
Copyright Renewed
All Rights in North America Administered by Blue Mountain Music Ltd./Irish Town Songs (ASCAP) and throughout the rest of the world by Blue Mountain Music Ltd. (PRS)

LAND OF A THOUSAND DANCES 🔊

Now try the D chord for this Wilson Pickett classic. Arch your fingers and play on the tips to avoid touching the other strings.

Na,   na, na, na, na,   na, na, na, na,   na, na, na, na, na, na.

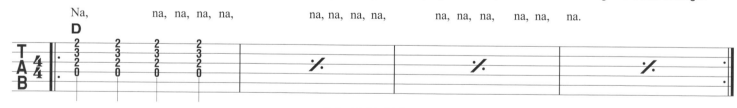

Words and Music by Chris Kenner
© 1963, 1970 (Renewed 1991) EMI LONGITUDE MUSIC

HEART OF GOLD 🔊

Let's practice changing between two chords with the intro from one of Neil Young's greatest hits.

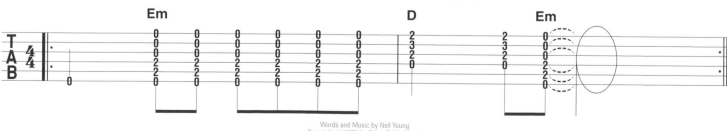

Words and Music by Neil Young
Copyright © 1971 by Silver Fiddle Music
Copyright Renewed

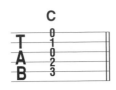
C

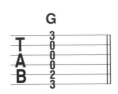
G

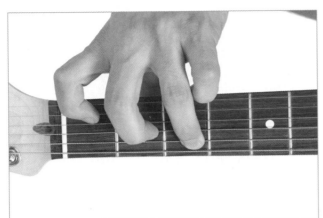

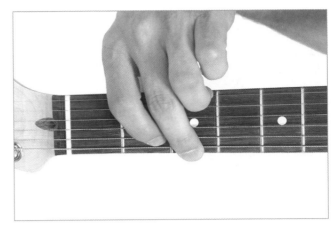

YELLOW SUBMARINE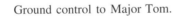

Try to keep a steady strum as you change chords for this all-time Beatles favorite.

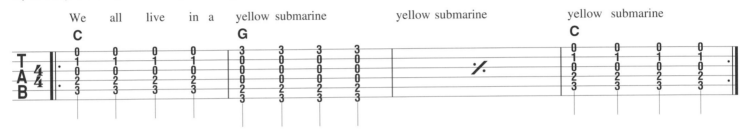

We all live in a yellow submarine   yellow submarine   yellow submarine

SPACE ODDITY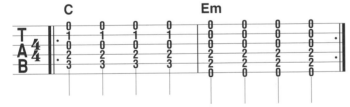

David Bowie used C and E minor chords at the beginning of the verse for this hit song.

Ground control to Major Tom.

SHOULD I STAY OR SHOULD I GO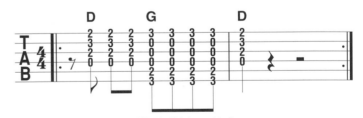

Open D and G chords kick off the intro of this classic by the Clash.

WONDERFUL TONIGHT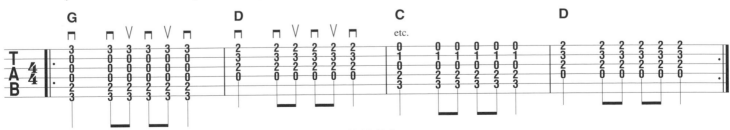

For Eric Clapton's "Wonderful Tonight," let's try a new strum pattern that uses both downstrokes ( ) and upstrokes ( ).

WILD NIGHT

Van Morrison's "Wild Night" is a certified rock classic and has been covered by numerous artists. It uses all four open chords introduced so far. Play the strum patterns written or feel free to try your own variations.

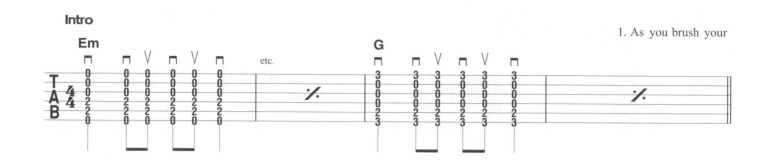

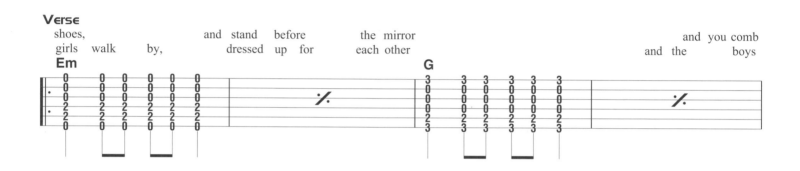

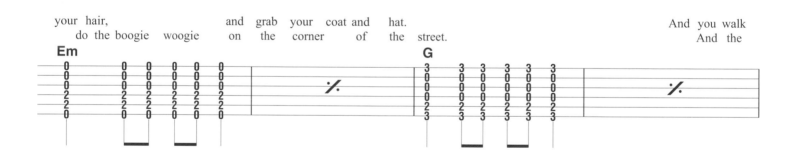

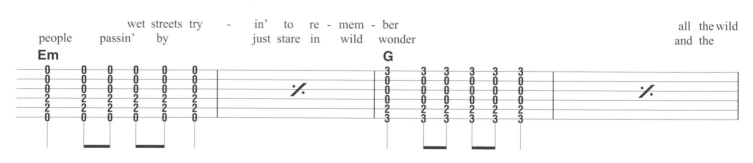

Words and Music by Van Morrison
© 1971 (Renewed) WB MUSIC CORP. and CALEDONIA SOUL MUSIC
All Rights Administered by WB MUSIC CORP.

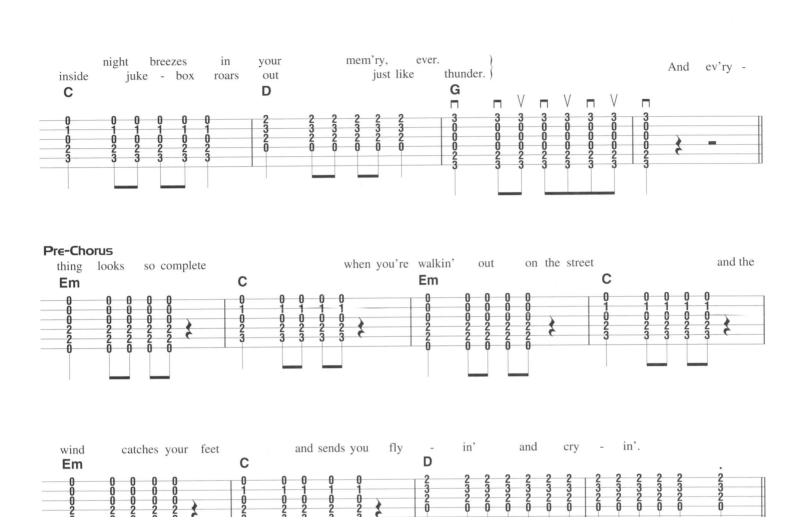

Pre-Chorus

thing looks so complete when you're walkin' out on the street and the

wind catches your feet and sends you fly - in' and cry - in'.

Chorus

Ooh, wee!

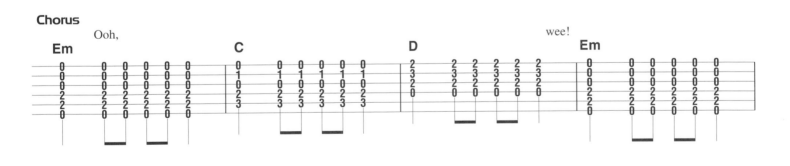

The wild night is calling.

1.

2. All the

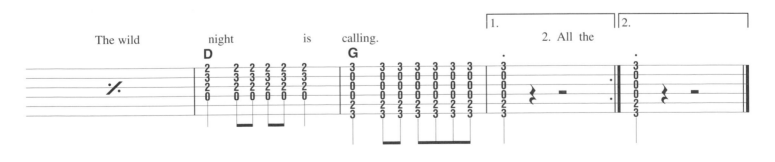

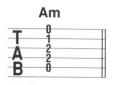

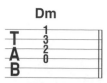

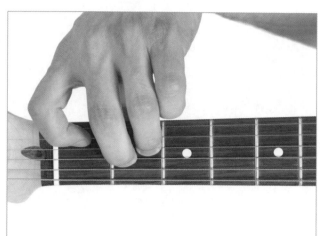

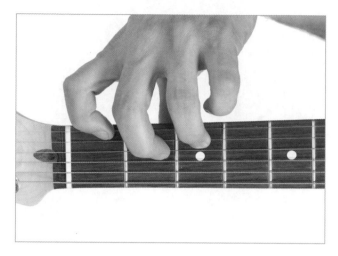

EVIL WAYS

Let's give your new A minor chord a workout with one of Santana's greatest hits. Listen to the audio to help you with the rhythms. Use the palm of your pick hand to silence the strings during the rests.

LOUIE, LOUIE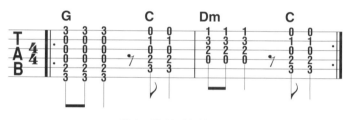

"Louie, Louie" is a rock 'n' roll standard and has been recorded by hundreds of artists. Its three-chord riff is instantly recognizable.

AIN'T NO SUNSHINE

Bill Withers' hit uses all three minor chords you've learned so far. It also incorporates two simple single notes.

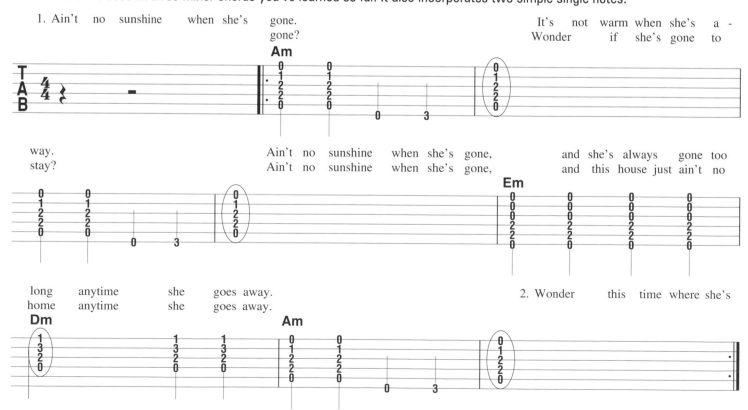

KNOCKIN' ON HEAVEN'S DOOR

Bob Dylan's timeless ballad uses open chords exclusively. Follow the strumming rhythms notated or just read the chord symbols and improvise your own strum patterns.

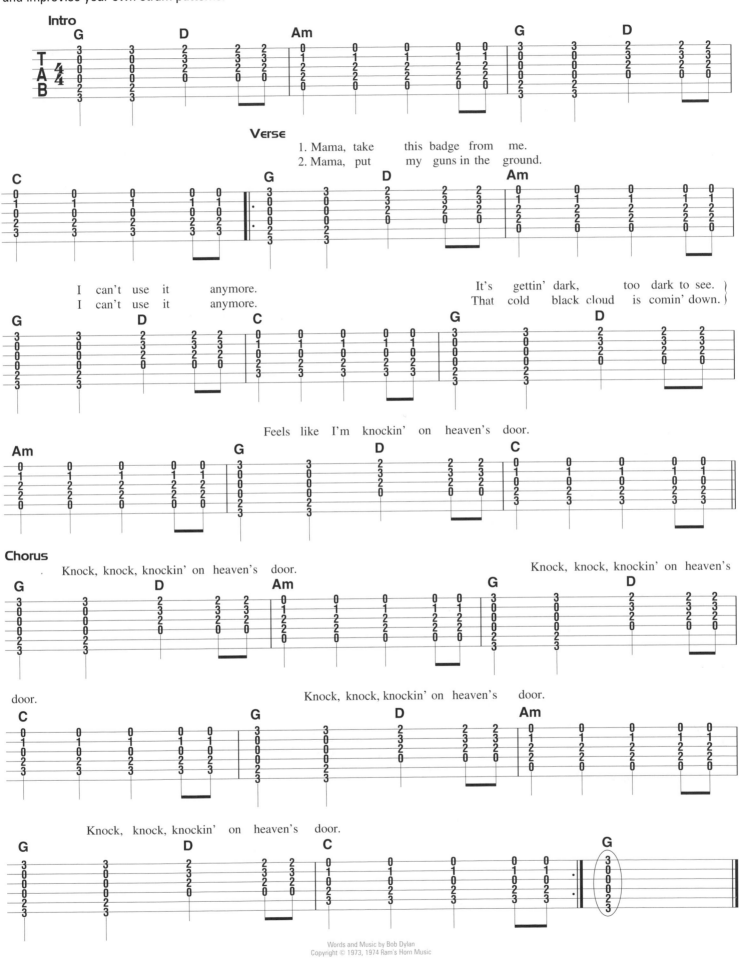

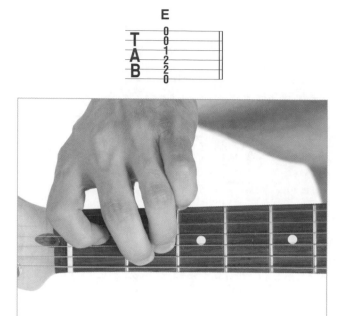

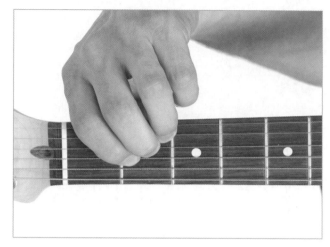

ABOUT A GIRL

For songs that change chords quickly, like this one by Nirvana, it's okay to release your fingers from one chord early in order to arrive at the next chord on time. It's natural for a few open strings to be struck in the transition.

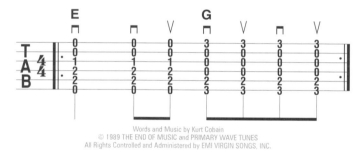

Words and Music by Kurt Cobain
© 1989 THE END OF MUSIC and PRIMARY WAVE TUNES
All Rights Controlled and Administered by EMI VIRGIN SONGS, INC.

R.O.C.K. IN THE U.S.A.

When using up/down strumming, don't worry about hitting every single string on the upstroke. It's okay to just play three or four notes of the chords, or whatever feels natural.

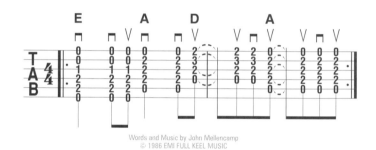

Words and Music by John Mellencamp
© 1986 EMI FULL KEEL MUSIC

BYE BYE LOVE

Another way to play an A chord is to lay your 1st finger across the top four strings at the 2nd fret. Many rock guitarists use this fingering and simply mute or miss the high E string. Experiment and choose which version works best for you in this hit by the Everly Brothers.

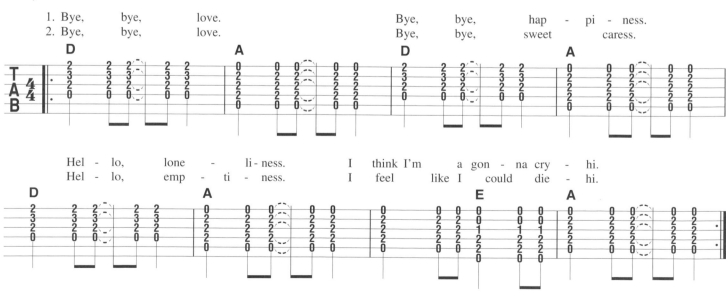

Words and Music by Felice Bryant and Boudleaux Bryant
Copyright © 1957 by HOUSE OF BRYANT PUBLICATIONS, Gatlinburg, TN
Copyright Renewed
All Foreign Rights Controlled by SONY/ATV MUSIC PUBLISHING LLC
All Rights for SONY/ATV MUSIC PUBLISHING LLC Administered by SONY/ATV MUSIC PUBLISHING LLC, 8 Music Square West, Nashville, TN 37203

PATIENCE

Here's a hit song by Guns N' Roses that uses five open chords.

Verse

1. Shed a tear 'cause I'm missin' you,   I'm still alright   to smile.
2. Was a time when I wasn't sure but you   set my mind   at ease.

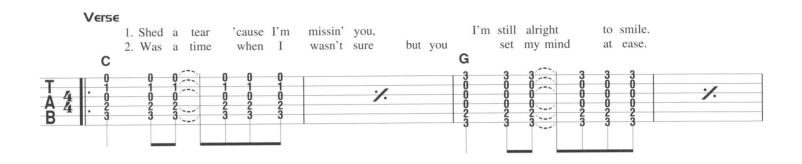

Girl, I think   about   you ev - 'ry   day   now.
There is no   doubt   you're in my   heart   now.

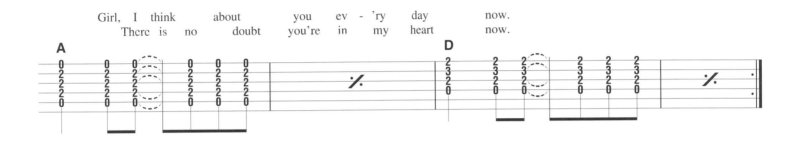

Chorus

Said, woman,   take it slow,   it'll work   itself   out fine.
Said, sugar,   make it slow,   and we come   togeth - er fine.

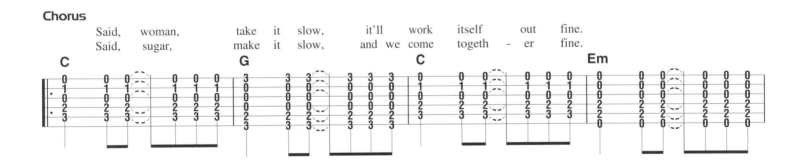

All we need is   just a lit - tle pa - tience.
All we need is   just a lit - tle pa - tience.

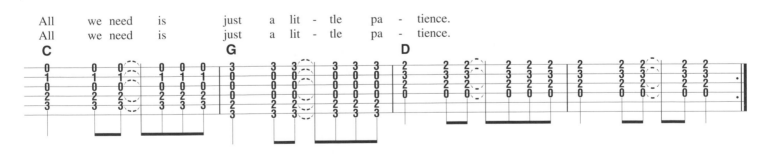

Words and Music by W. Axl Rose, Slash, Izzy Stradlin', Duff McKagan and Steven Adler
Copyright © 1988 Guns N' Roses Music (ASCAP) and Black Frog Music (ASCAP)
All Rights for Black Frog Music in the U.S. and Canada Controlled and Administered by Universal - PolyGram International Publishing, Inc.

SLIDES, HAMMER-ONS & PULL-OFFS

Sometimes, it's not so much what you play, it's how you play it. In music terms, this is called **articulation**. Slides, hammer-ons, and pull-offs all belong to a special category of articulations called **legato**. Legato techniques allow you to connect two or more consecutive notes together to create a smooth, flowing sound.

To play a **slide**, pick the first note as you normally would. Then, maintain pressure as you move your fret-hand finger up or down the fretboard to sound the second note. (The second note is not picked.) In tab, a slide is indicated with a short, slanted line and a curved **slur**.

MY SHARONA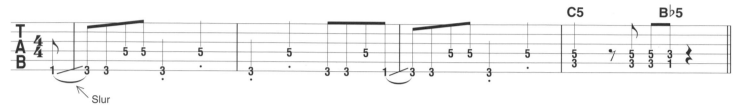

Use your 1st finger to do the sliding for this riff by the Knack.

BOOM BOOM

Now try this John Lee Hooker blues riff. The slide is played with the 3rd finger. This allows your 2nd finger to play the notes on the 3rd fret and your 1st finger to play the notes on the 2nd fret.

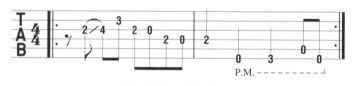

SWEET LEAF

Chords can also be connected by slides. Here is a classic heavy metal riff by the band Black Sabbath.

To play a **hammer-on**, pick the first note and then press down, or "hammer on" to, a higher note along the same string. The initial attack should carry the tone over both notes.

LIFE IN THE FAST LANE

Here's a famous guitar intro by the Eagles. Use your 1st finger to play the notes on the 2nd fret.

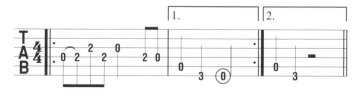

PAPERBACK WRITER

For this Beatles riff, lay your 1st finger across the bottom three strings at the 3rd fret. Maintain pressure as you use your 3rd and 4th fingers to play the notes on the 5th fret.

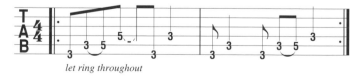

let ring throughout

A **pull-off** is the opposite of a hammer-on. First, start with both fingers planted. Pick the higher note, then tug or "pull" that finger off the string to sound the lower note, which is already fretted by the lower finger.

BRING IT ON HOME

This riff by Led Zeppelin features pull-offs on the 3rd string.

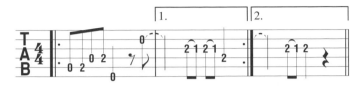

CULT OF PERSONALITY

Notes can also be pulled off to open strings, as this riff by Living Colour demonstrates.

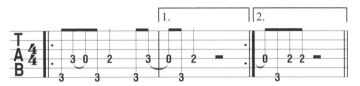

Of course, slides, hammer-ons, and pull-offs can be used in any combination. Here are a few examples.

THE MAN WHO SOLD THE WORLD

This David Bowie song was famously covered by Nirvana on MTV's *Unplugged*. For the back-to-back hammer-pull in the 2nd measure, only the first of the three notes is picked.

COME OUT AND PLAY

The Offspring's "Come Out and Play" contains hammer-ons and slides. The first part of the slide occurs very quickly and is called a **grace-note slide**.

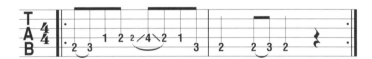

BLUEGRASS RUN

Legato articulations are common in all styles of guitar music. Here's a fun bluegrass lick that uses all three types of slurs introduced so far.

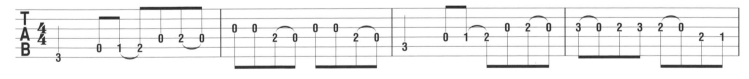

HEY JOE

What better way to wrap up this book than with one of Jimi Hendrix's biggest hits. "Hey Joe" contains several chords, single notes on all six strings, slides, hammer-ons, and more!

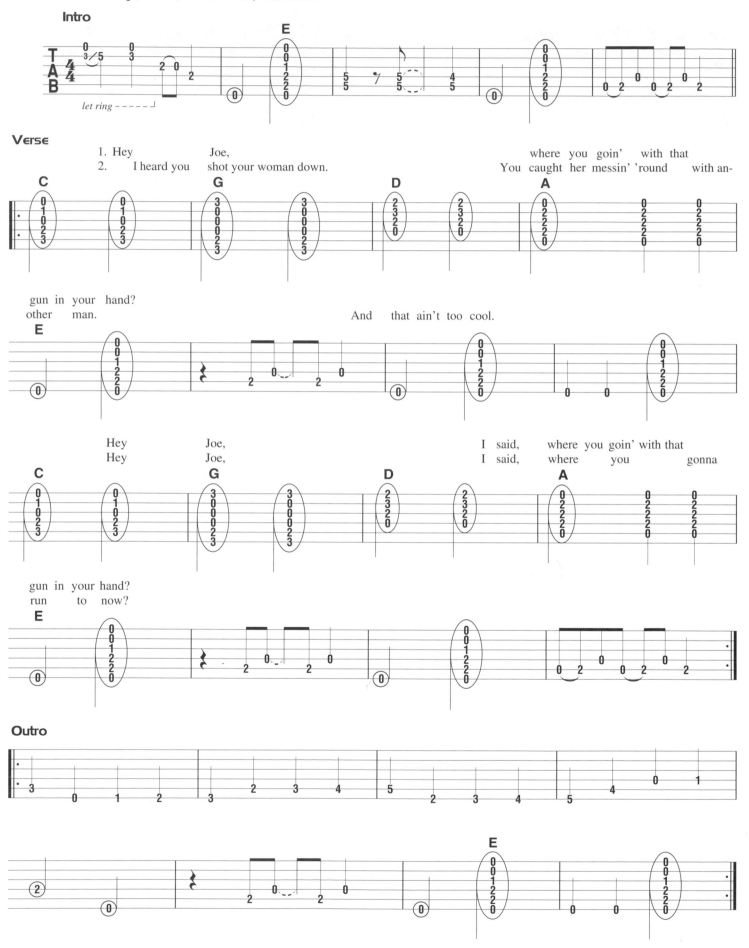